SUGAR & SPICE

with Jo Seagar

A SELECTION OF THE BEST RECIPES FROM
THE CHELSEA SUGAR
GREAT NEW ZEALAND BAKE-OFF

RANDOM HOUSE
NEW ZEALAND

Grateful acknowledgement is made to the
following suppliers of photographic props:

Country Road
Epicurean Workshop
Freedom Furniture
Living & Giving
Milly's Kitchen Shop
nest
Redcurrant
Studio Ceramics
The Garden Party
Theme Basics Kitchenware
The Store

New Zealand Sugar Company Limited,
P O Box 30, Birkenhead, Auckland 1015, New Zealand
email: chelsea@nzsugar.co.nz
www.chelsea.co.nz

A RANDOM HOUSE BOOK
published by
Random House New Zealand
18 Poland Road, Glenfield, Auckland, New Zealand
www.randomhouse.co.nz

First published 2000. Reprinted 2001, 2007, 2011
© 2000 New Zealand Sugar Company Limited

ISBN 978 1 86941 438 2
Introductions, tips and selection: Jo Seagar
Jo's foodie team: Annabelle Ullrich and Brenda Legg
Design: Christine Cathie
Layout: Graeme Leather
Photography: Shaun Cato-Symonds
Printed in China by Everbest Printing Co Ltd

CONTENTS

INTRODUCTION

We've had the most wonderful response to our Chelsea Sugar Great New Zealand Bake-Off competition. It appears that no one in this country, even the strongest willed, can resist the smell of fresh baking wafting out of the kitchen.

There have been thousands of fabulous entries. All manner of treasured 'secret' recipes from old hand-me-down favourites of Grandma's, lovingly prepared generation after generation, to spectacular new contemporary 'inventions'. Some have resulted out of culinary disasters, where a certain ingredient had to be substituted half-way through the cooking process or where recipes were mis-interpreted, measurements got wrong and even power failures that turned a quick-cook, high-temperature muffin into a slow-baked gooey pud. When one of these new breed of recipes evolve, the original is nearly always ditched in favour of the new 'family favourite'.

Personally, I have thoroughly enjoyed working my way through the mountains of entries, reading the stories and sharing the history of each recipe. The appeal of nostalgia has been a huge draw-card for me and many times I have been taken back to my own childhood through sharing the memories of others.

In this book, we present our top choices for each section. It was a very difficult, closely fought selection process made from vast piles of possibilities. The testing and re-testing has been weeks' worth of work (and pleasure!). Some recipes we have fiddled with, refining ingredients and making changes to the measurements to fit modern metric-sized cups and cake tins – old ounces and pounds have been converted to grams and, wherever possible, to easy-to-use cups and spoons. There is still plenty of room for your own personal innovation with each recipe, so feel free to substitute different fruits or icings and even add extra chocolate here and there, if you so desire. You can put your own mark on these recipes and customise them to suit your individual tastes.

This book is all about both old-fashioned flavours in great new presentations and snazzy innovations bursting with taste-bud surprises. This is home cooking at its best, preparing delicious food for the ones we love. Food that is good to eat, easy to prepare and familiar to everyone. It is the sort of thing Mum used to make, only better! Your biggest problem will be stopping the fights over who gets the last delicious morsel and who gets to lick the bowl at clean-up time.

Happy cooking, New Zealand!

Jo Seagar

BISCUITS & SLICES

Left: Crispy Cracknels

I achieve great personal joy in baking biscuits and slices for my family, and it's obvious from the entries sent in that more and more people are also revelling in the simple pleasure of this hands-on area of cooking. Delicious biscuits and slices open the floodgates on food memories and make you feel like a kid again – a kid who yearns for your mother's home-baked goodies and those gorgeous accompanying smells wafting out of the kitchen.

The range across this section is vast. There are sumptuously sticky and rich slices and healthy crispy oat biscuits.

Some recipes date back years and some are clever new innovations.

The accompanying stories have been such fun to read. Lots of naughty boys pinching bickies off the cooling rack and school-holiday midnight raids on the tins. I encourage you to have a go at cooking something from this biscuit and slice collection as the results will be more economical and taste so much nicer than store-bought treats. You'll certainly be putting happy smiles on faces in your home.

Jo Seagar

'Bloody Good' Fudge Slice

MAKES 25–30 PIECES

150 g butter
2 tablespoons Chelsea golden syrup
1 cup Chelsea white sugar
1 cup coconut
1 tablespoon cocoa
2 cups flour
1 cup sultanas
$^1/_2$–1 cup chopped walnuts

In a large saucepan or microwave bowl melt the butter, add the golden syrup, then add the dry ingredients, mixing well. Press into a well-greased or paper-lined slice or sponge-roll tray and bake for 10 minutes at 150°C. Ice when cool with chocolate frosting or melted chocolate.

Chocolate Frosting
2 cups Chelsea icing sugar
3 heaped tablespoons cocoa
25 g butter melted
boiling water

Mix all ingredients, adding enough boiling water to make a smooth paste. Spread over cooled slice and cut into squares.

THIS RECIPE ACQUIRED ITS NAME WHEN MY HUSBAND WAS ABOUT 3 YEARS OLD. HIS MUM HAD MADE A BATCH AND SOME NEW-FOUND FRIENDS THOUGHT 'IT WAS BLOODY GOOD!' THE FRIENDS TURNED OUT TO BE TELECOM LINESMEN WORKING UP THE ROAD.

Nikki Marsh of Beachhaven, Auckland

Lemon Kisses

Top half

1 egg white
1 teaspoon cold water
1 cup Chelsea caster sugar

Beat egg white with cold water, until stiff. Slowly add sugar and beat until thick and glossy. Pipe out or put small spoonfuls in little peaks the size of a 20-cent coin on an oven tray lined with baking paper. Bake at 120°C for 30–35 minutes until they easily lift off the paper. They should remain creamy-white like a meringue. These will keep for 2 weeks in an airtight container.

Bottom half

1 egg
1 egg yolk
1 teaspoon cold water
$1/2$ cup (100 g) Chelsea caster sugar
$1/2$ cup (100 g) flour
$1/2$ teaspoon baking powder

Beat egg and extra yolk with cold water. Stir in sugar, flour and baking powder. Roll into little balls the same size as the top halves and press flat on a well-greased or baking-paper-lined oven tray. Bake for 10 minutes at 200°C and cool on a wire rack. These will firm up as they cool and can be kept for 2 weeks in an airtight container. Join the tops and bottoms together with whipped cream or a little lemon curd (see recipe page 46) and cream.

MY MOTHER-IN-LAW GAVE ME THIS RECIPE ABOUT 46 YEARS AGO. SHE ALWAYS HAD A PLATE OF THEM TO TAKE TO COUNTRY DANCES. THEY CAN BE MADE IN ADVANCE AND FILLED BEFORE EATING.

Lemon Marshmallow Slice

MAKES 20 PIECES

Filling

1 cup Chelsea white sugar
1 cup water
juice and grated rind 2 lemons
$^1/_2$ cup milk
2 tablespoons custard powder
2 tablespoons cornflour

Put sugar, water and the juice and rind of the lemons in a saucepan and bring to the boil. Separately mix the milk, custard powder and cornflour to a smooth paste. Stir the 2 mixtures together using a wire whisk, then slowly bring to the boil and boil for 3 minutes. Pour over the shortcake.

Marshmallow

2 tablespoons gelatine
1 cup boiling water
1 cup Chelsea white sugar
1 teaspoon lemon essence
1 cup Chelsea icing sugar

In a medium-large saucepan dissolve gelatine in the water. Add the sugar and boil for 8 minutes, then cool. Add the lemon essence and icing sugar and beat until thick and creamy. Pour at once over the filling and leave to set. Cut when cold.

Shortcake

125 g butter
$^3/_4$ cup Chelsea icing sugar
1 egg beaten
$1^1/_2$ cups self-raising flour
$^1/_2$ teaspoon vanilla essence

Cream butter and sugar. Add egg, flour, and vanilla essence. Mix well then press into a well-greased slice or sponge-roll tray. Bake for 15–20 minutes at 160°C until pale golden coloured. Cool.

Raewyn McLean of Taupiri

Crispy Cracknels

MAKES APPROX. 30

These biscuits should be a fairly pale golden colour. They keep extremely well in an airtight container and make wonderful presents.

1 cup flour
1 teaspoon baking powder
pinch salt
50 g butter
1 cup Chelsea white sugar
1 cup medium-cut coconut (not fine)
1 large egg
optional topping (see tips)

Put flour, baking powder, salt and butter into a food processor and mix well. Add sugar, then process until just mixed. Add coconut and pulse to just mix through. Break egg into the food processor and run the machine until the dough clumps together around the blade.

With floured hands, roll the dough into a sausage-shaped log approx. 2.5 cm thick and slice into little discs. Press the discs flat on a baking-paper-lined or well-greased oven tray. If you wish, you can top with your chosen flavouring. Bake at 160°C for 10–12 minutes. The biscuits tend to puff up then sink when they come out of the oven. Rest for 2 minutes on the tray before removing to cool thoroughly (and crisp up) on a wire rack.

MY MOTHER SENT THESE TO HER BROTHER DURING THE WAR WHEN HE WAS WITH THE ARMY IN ITALY AND THEY KEPT BEAUTIFULLY. IN FACT, KEPT IN AN AIRTIGHT CONTAINER THEY SEEM TO KEEP FOR EVER.

JO SEAGAR'S TIPS

A clear winner for its lasting crispness, easy method and having so much room for innovation. The optional topping could be Mrs Thornton's favourite of finely chopped crystallised ginger, but mixed peel, chocolate chips, chopped nuts, coffee crystals or hundred and thousands could be used instead. At Christmas, green and red glacé cherries look great.

Connor Coconut Squares

MAKES **20** PIECES

125 g butter
$^1/_2$ cup Chelsea white sugar
1 teaspoon Chelsea golden syrup
1 cup flour
1 cup desiccated coconut
1 teaspoon baking powder

Cream butter, sugar and golden syrup.
Add other ingredients and mix. Press into
a greased slice tray. Bake until golden at
180°C (about 20–25 minutes). Cool before
icing.

Icing

1 cup Chelsea icing sugar
1 cup desiccated coconut
$^1/_4$ can condensed milk
1 teaspoon cocoa
30 g butter

Heat all the ingredients until melted and
well blended. Spread on cooled slice. Cut
into squares. Store in an airtight
container.

JO SEAGAR'S TIPS

You could substitute the cocoa icing flavouring with coffee or butterscotch or even
peppermint. Try colouring the coconut in the
icing with a few drops of food colouring for
special occasions.

THIS RECIPE WAS GIVEN TO ME OVER 40 YEARS
AGO. IT IS A GREAT FAMILY FAVOURITE.

Janet Connor of Dunedin

Sultana Jammy Puffs

MAKES 12

1 cup sultanas
$^1/_2$ cup Chelsea soft brown sugar
1 tablespoon raspberry or blackberry jam
3 sheets flaky puff pastry
$^1/_4$ cup milk
$^1/_4$ cup Chelsea white sugar

In a food processor place the sultanas, brown sugar and jam. Blend well. Cut 12 x 9 cm rounds out of the pastry (approx. the top of a coffee mug). Place 1 teaspoon of sultana mix into centre of each (don't be tempted to add more than 1 teaspoon). Start from one side and begin folding edge into centre of pastry. Work around until all the edges are folded into the centre covering the filling. Place milk in a saucer and white sugar in another. Dip smooth side of pastry into milk, shake, then dip into the sugar. Place sugar side up on a well-greased or baking-paper-lined oven tray.

Bake for 15–20 minutes at 190°C. Cool on a wire rack before eating, as the filling is boiling hot.

NANA O'S QUICK RECIPE. THE PUFFS ARE EASY TO MAKE AND LOOK VERY IMPRESSIVE.

Gillian Pennefather of Wellsford

Graham's Sultana Biscuits (right) and Ginger Crinkle Biscuits

Graham's Sultana Biscuits

125 g butter
$^{1}/_{2}$ cup Chelsea white sugar
2 tablespoons milk
1 dessertspoon Chelsea golden syrup
1 teaspoon baking soda
1 $^{3}/_{4}$ cups flour
$^{1}/_{2}$ cup sultanas
1 teaspoon vanilla essence

THIS FAMILY FAVOURITE OF OVER 50 YEARS GOT ITS NAME BECAUSE MY BROTHER GRAHAM WOULD EAT MY MOTHER'S BISCUITS ON A DAILY BASIS. WHEN I MARRIED AND HAD A 'GRAHAM' OF MY OWN, THESE BISCUITS BECAME HIS FAVOURITE TOO.

In a large saucepan melt butter, then add sugar, milk, syrup and soda, mixing until it fizzes. Remove from heat and leave to cool. Stir in the flour, sultanas and vanilla essence. Mix well.

Roll into little golf balls and place on a well-greased or baking-paper-lined tray. Press down with a wet fork. Bake for 10–15 minutes at 160°C. Leave on the baking tray for 1 minute then carefully remove to a wire rack to cool. Store in an airtight container.

Ginger Crinkle Biscuits

MAKES 36

²/₃ cup oil

1 cup Chelsea white sugar

1 egg

¹/₄ cup Chelsea treacle

2 cups flour

2 teaspoons baking soda

2 teaspoons ground cinnamon

1 teaspoon ground ginger

¹/₄ cup Chelsea white sugar to roll
   biscuits in

Preheat oven to 180°C. Beat oil, sugar, egg and treacle together. Stir in flour, baking soda and spices, mix well. Drop teaspoonfuls into the sugar and form balls. Place on ungreased baking tray 5 cm apart. Bake for 10–15 minutes, then carefully remove to cool on a wire rack and store in an airtight container. These cookies flatten and crinkle all by themselves.

THIS IS A RECIPE MY MOTHER USED WHEN I WAS LITTLE. BECAUSE OF THE OIL, THIS IS A **MORE HEALTHY** SORT OF BISCUIT. THE SUGAR PLUS TREACLE GIVE THE BISCUIT ITS **UNIQUE** DARK, RICH COLOUR AND SWEET TASTE.

Shirley Bradstock of Christchurch

Slugs

250 g butter
90 g (approx. $^{1}/_{4}$ cup) Chelsea white sugar
1 egg
250 g (2 cups) flour
1 tablespoon coconut
1 teaspoon cream of tartar
1 teaspoon baking soda
extra coconut (approx. $^{1}/_{2}$ cup)
icing sugar for dusting

Cream the butter and sugar. Add beaten egg. Add flour mixed with coconut, cream of tartar and baking soda. Roll the mixture into a sausage shape, then roll this in the extra coconut sprinkled on a board. Cut into 4 cm lengths. Place on a well-greased or baking-paper-lined oven tray.

Bake until golden at 150°C for approx. 20 minutes. Cool on a wire rack. Join together with butter icing. Store in an airtight container.

Butter Icing
1$^{1}/_{2}$ cups Chelsea icing sugar
25 g butter melted
2 tablespoons milk
few drops vanilla essence

Mix all the ingredients together into a smooth spreadable butter consistency.

THIS HAS BEEN A FAMILY FAVOURITE EVER SINCE MY SCOTTISH GRANDMOTHER CAME TO NEW ZEALAND AS A WORLD WAR I BRIDE.

Judy Burrows of Murupara

Slugs (on back of plate) and Coffee Crystal Biscuits

Coffee Crystal Biscuits

MAKES APPROX. 24

Base

$1^1/_4$ cups (200 g) flour

150 g butter

$^1/_3$ cup (100 g) Chelsea caster sugar

$^1/_2$ teaspoon baking powder

1 teaspoon cinnamon

Mix all ingredients together in a food processor or mixer until they clump together in a ball. On a floured board roll out to a square about $^1/_2$ cm thick.

Topping

2 tablespoons coffee crystals

2 tablespoons finely chopped almonds

Mix crystals and almonds and sprinkle over the rolled-out dough. Roll very lightly with a rolling pin to press topping mix into the dough. Cut into fingers or squares and place on a well-greased or baking-paper-lined oven tray. Bake for 20 minutes at 180°C. Cool on a wire rack.

JO SEAGAR'S TIPS

For an alternative topping you could use chocolate chips, coarsely chopped chocolate (even white chocolate), toasted pecans or hazelnuts, finely chopped crystallised ginger, macadamia halves or sliced almonds. Of course they could be iced or simply dusted with cinnamon mixed with icing sugar. These will make great gifts.

Margaretha Bell of Rotorua

Nellie's Louisa Cake

MAKES APPROX. 36 PIECES

Base

125 g butter
³/₄ cup Chelsea white sugar
1 egg
1³/₄ cups flour
2 teaspoons baking powder
approx. 1 cup raspberry jam

Cream butter and sugar, then add egg and mix well. Stir in flour and baking powder. Press into a well-greased or paper-lined roasting dish (26 x 30 cm at the base) or 2 slice trays. Spread with raspberry jam.

Topping

1 cup coconut
1 cup Chelsea white sugar
1 egg

Mix all topping ingredients together well and then spread over the jam-covered base. Bake for 30–40 minutes at 165°C. Cool in the tin then cut into pieces.

A GREAT FAVOURITE OF MINE WHEN I WAS A CHILD, IT CONTINUES AS A FAVOURITE WITH MY CHILDREN AND ALL 20 OF MY GRANDCHILDREN. IT CAN BE READY FROM 'GO TO WHOA' IN 45 MINUTES AND WILL PROVIDE ENOUGH FOR A GOOD BIG GATHERING. OUR FAMILY ALWAYS CALLS THIS LOUISA CAKE NOT JUST PLAIN LOUISE CAKE.

Rich Plum Slice

Base

125 g butter

1/2 cup Chelsea white sugar

1 egg

grated rind 1 lemon

2 cups self-raising flour

1 x 425 g can whole plums in syrup

Cream butter and sugar. Add egg, grated lemon rind and flour and mix well. Pour into well-greased or paper-lined slice or sponge-roll tray and spread out evenly. Cut plums in half and remove stones. Arrange plum halves over pastry base, pressing gently into the mixture.

JO SEAGAR'S TIPS

This recipe works just as well with peaches, plums, pears and even fresh strawberries. Use it as a basic shortcake slice and customise with whatever fruit you fancy.

Topping

60 g butter

4 tablespoons Chelsea white sugar

6 tablespoons flour

Mix together all the topping ingredients then sprinkle over plums. Bake for 30–45 minutes at 180°C. Cool in tin before cutting into slices.

Angela Goodman of Palmerston North

Granny's Scrumptious Coffee and Date Fingers

2 eggs
1 cup Chelsea soft brown sugar
175 g butter melted
$^1/_2$ cup milk
1 tablespoon sweetened coffee essence
1 cup dates finely chopped
$1^1/_2$ cups flour
2 teaspoons baking powder

Beat eggs, add the remaining ingredients and mix well to thoroughly combine. Spread into a well-greased or baking-paper-lined slice or sponge-roll tray. Bake for 30 minutes at 150°C. Cool in the tray. Ice with coffee icing, cut into squares or fingers.

Coffee Icing
2 cups Chelsea icing sugar
25 g butter melted
1 tablespoon sweetened coffee essence
boiling water

Mix all icing ingredients together, adding enough boiling water until a smooth, spreadable icing forms.

JO SEAGAR'S TIPS

The coffee and date combination is scrumptious but chocolate and date slice with chocky icing is equally delicious: just add 2 tablespoons of cocoa to the base and icing recipes.

Phyllis Hogg of Timaru

Quick Custard Squares with Passionfruit Icing

MAKES APPROX. 20 SQUARES

24 plain square water cracker biscuits
  e.g. (Huntley and Palmers)
$^1/_2$ cup custard powder
$2^1/_2$ cups milk
$^1/_2$ cup Chelsea white sugar
$^1/_2$ teaspoon vanilla essence

Use 12 square crackers to line a 20 x 24 cm dish. Cut crackers with serrated knife to fit if necessary. Mix custard powder to a smooth paste with a little of the milk. Separately heat the rest of the milk, then add the sugar. With a wire whisk, stir in the custard powder paste and continue to heat and stir until boiling and thickened. Remove from heat and add vanilla essence, then pour custard over crackers. Top with remaining crackers, leave until cool, then refrigerate until quite cold and set.

Icing

2 cups Chelsea icing sugar
25 g butter melted
2–3 tablespoons passionfruit pulp

Combine icing sugar and butter with passionfruit pulp and mix until smooth. Spread over cooled crackers after they've set. Cut into squares when set.

Robyn Alexander of Napier

Peanut Drops

MAKES APPROX. 25

150 g butter
$^1/_2$ cup Chelsea white sugar
1 teaspoon vanilla essence
1 cup self-raising flour
1 cup shelled roasted peanuts, preferably
  unsalted

Cream butter and sugar. Add vanilla essence, flour and peanuts. Drop teaspoonfuls onto a well-greased or baking-paper-lined tray. Bake for 15 minutes at 180°C. Allow to cool a few minutes on the tray before removing to further cool on a wire rack. Store in an airtight container.

JO SEAGAR'S TIPS

This is like a 'blond' peanut brownie and already the favourite bickie with my 2 children. Easy to substitute macadamia or almonds for a smart occasion and so quick to make!

CAKES

Left: Soonafai's Moist Chocky Cake

Wonderful cakes have been a mainstay of everyday cooking since early settlement times. Here are some lovely heritage recipes for guaranteed baking success every time. Lots of entrants told of how they'd been given the original versions of their recipes by their mothers and grandmothers and how they'd survived the test of time and the demanding tastes of successive generations.

Not surprisingly, we've had over 400 entries for the ever-popular chocolate cake, so the final decision-making was very difficult. However, I think you'll agree when you try Soonafai's Moist Chocky Cake that we have a fabulous winner. So many of the entries for cakes, and especially the chocolate cakes, were the same recipe and obviously a good one at that, but Soonafai's is just that extra bit special and different. It makes a big perfect cake every time and it's simple and quick to prepare with ingredients you'd find in the store cupboard.

There are some wonderful new combinations and surprises among the entries. I encourage you to try the cucumber cake – it may just push the perennial carrot cake off its pedestal. From moist and scrumptiously fruity to farmhouse classics to gooey and fudgy – this collection covers the whole spectrum.

Jo Seagar

Prune and Coconut Dream Cake

MAKES VERY LARGE CAKE

2 cups water (or 1$^{1}/_{2}$ cups water, $^{1}/_{2}$ cup
   green ginger wine)

2 cups prunes and/or plump dried
   apricots

2 tablespoons baking soda

3 cups flour

2$^{1}/_{2}$ cups Chelsea caster sugar

250 g butter

2 eggs

2 teaspoons vanilla essence

2 cups peeled and diced apple

Topping

1$^{1}/_{3}$ cups Chelsea soft brown sugar

120 g butter

2 cups shredded desiccated coconut

175 ml milk

Bring water to the boil. Add prunes and/or apricots and simmer 2 minutes. Add baking soda. In large bowl mix all other ingredients thoroughly. Pour into a well-greased or baking-paper-lined deep 30 cm cake tin. Bake for 1$^{1}/_{2}$ hours at 150°C.

Mix all the topping ingredients in a saucepan until butter has melted. Pour on top of the cake and bake for a further 30 minutes (may need more) until golden coloured and set.

Old English Gingerbread

500 g (4 cups) self-raising flour

1 teaspoon salt

1 tablespoon ground ginger

1 tablespoon baking powder

1$^1/_2$ cups Chelsea soft brown sugar

175 g butter

5 tablespoons Chelsea treacle

5 tablespoons Chelsea golden syrup

300 ml milk

2 eggs

1 tablespoon warm milk to mix

1 teaspoon bicarbonate of soda

1 teaspoon cinnamon

2 tablespoons approx. Chelsea demerara or
  raw sugar

Sift together flour, salt, ginger and baking powder. In a saucepan, warm sugar, butter, treacle and golden syrup. In a separate pan, warm the 300 ml of milk and beat in eggs. Combine with flour and syrup mixtures and mix thoroughly. Mix tablespoon of warm milk and bicarbonate soda together, then add to the mixture. Put into a 25 cm square, well-greased or baking-paper-lined cake tin. Mix the cinnamon with the demerara or raw sugar and sprinkle on the top. Bake for 1$^1/_2$ hours (or until firm) at 180°C.

THIS IS A RECIPE GIVEN TO ME BY AN ELDERLY FRIEND IN 1963. HER MOTHER GAVE IT TO HER IN THE EARLY 1900S. IT HAS HAD A FEW CHANGES, GIVEN THAT IT'S NO LONGER COOKED IN A COAL RANGE, BUT IS STILL A GREAT FAVOURITE – A GOOD 'CUT AND COME AGAIN CAKE' LOVELY PLAIN OR SLICED WITH A LITTLE BUTTER.

Pat Pepperell of Nelson

Moist Fruit Cake (with no eggs)

MAKES LARGE FAMILY CAKE

125 g butter
1¹/₂ cups Chelsea white sugar
2 cups milk
400–500 g dried fruit mix
1¹/₂ cups self-raising flour
1¹/₂ cups wheaten cornflour
1 teaspoon cinnamon
1 teaspoon baking soda
1 teaspoon mixed spice
1 teaspoon salt

Boil butter, sugar, milk and fruit in a saucepan for 5 minutes. When cool, mix in rest of ingredients. Pour into well-greased or baking-paper-lined 23 cm cake tin. Bake for 1³/₄–2 hours at 160°C.

Naomi Jury of Remuera, Auckland

Macadamia Orange Pumpkin Cake

MAKES LARGE CAKE

300 g butter
1 cup Chelsea soft brown sugar
2 tablespoons grated orange rind
4 eggs
3 cups grated pumpkin
$^{1}/_{2}$ cup macadamia nuts finely chopped
2 cups flour
2 teaspoons cinnamon
1 teaspoon mixed spice
4 teaspoons baking powder
$^{1}/_{2}$ cup milk approx.
4 tablespoons oil

Sour Cream Orange Frosting

3 cups Chelsea icing sugar approx.
4 tablespoons sour cream
2 teaspoons grated orange rind
small amount of orange juice
optional orange liqueur e.g. Cointreau or
   Grand Marnier
toasted macadamia nuts for decoration

Cream butter, sugar and orange rind, add eggs and beat in well. Add the remaining ingredients and mix well to combine.

Pour mixture into two well-greased or baking-paper-lined 20–22 cm cake tins. Bake for 35–40 minutes at 175°C. Cool on a wire rack.

Blend all icing ingredients except macadamia nuts until you get a spreadable consistency (if desired add a splash of orange liqueur). Frost one cake then place other cake on top and cover with remaining frosting. Sprinkle with chopped macadamia nuts (or alternative nuts).

Quick 'n' Easy Feijoa Cake

$^1/_2$ cup milk

2 eggs

$1^1/_4$ cups Chelsea white sugar

1 cup mashed feijoas

1 teaspoon vanilla essence

75 g butter

Place above ingredients in a food processor and mix until smooth.

2 cups flour

1 teaspoon baking powder

1 teaspoon baking soda

$^1/_2$ teaspoon salt

Pour the processor contents into a bowl with the remaining ingredients and mix well. Pour into a well-greased or baking-paper-lined 20–23 cm cake tin. Bake for 40–45 minutes at 180°C. Ice if desired.

JO SEAGAR'S TIPS

This cake is superb topped with lemon butter icing

2 cups Chelsea icing sugar
grated rind and juice 1 lemon
25 g butter melted

Mix all ingredients together until smooth. Add extra lemon juice if required to make a fluffy butter consistency.

Elizabeth Gunson of Ongaonga

Soonafai's Moist Chocky Cake

MAKES DEEP AVERAGE-SIZED
CAKE

2 cups Chelsea caster sugar

3 cups self-raising flour

2 teaspoons baking soda

$^1/_2$ cup cocoa

3 eggs, separated

2 cups milk

2 tablespoons malt vinegar

2 tablespoons Chelsea golden syrup

2 teaspoons vanilla

$1^1/_2$ cups cooking oil, eg Canola

1 egg

whipped cream and icing of your choice
  for finishing cake

Combine all dry ingredients. In a large bowl, beat the 3 egg whites until stiff. In a separate bowl, combine milk and vinegar, then add the rest of the wet ingredients, including the whole egg and 3 egg yolks, and beat. Mix wet and dry ingredients together, then fold in the beaten egg whites. Pour into two well-greased or baking-paper-lined cake tins about 20–23 cm. Bake for 25–30 minutes at 180°C. Cool on a wire rack. To serve, pile whipped cream on one cake, place the other cake on top and ice – try chocolate frosting (see page 9).

AFTER SEVERAL ATTEMPTS AT CHANGING A RECIPE THAT WASN'T VERY NICE, AND WITH THE FAMILY AS TESTERS, I CAME UP WITH THIS LOVELY MOIST CHOCKY CAKE LOVED BY EVERYONE.

Soonafai Fesolai of Kelston, Auckland

No Measure Chocnut Cake

MAKES AVERAGE-SIZED CAKE

250 g tub sour cream
3 eggs
1 tub chopped walnuts
1 tub milo
1 tub flour
1 tub Chelsea white sugar
1 teaspoon baking powder
$^{1}/_{2}$ teaspoon salt
1 teaspoon vanilla
$^{1}/_{2}$ tub oil

Preheat oven to 160°C. Empty tub of sour cream into bowl and stir until smooth. Wash and dry tub to use as a measure. Add eggs, mix and put aside. Chop up walnuts until they resemble coarse breadcrumbs. Place walnuts and remaining ingredients into a clean large bowl and stir. Add the sour cream and egg mixture and mix. Pour into a well-greased or baking-paper-lined 23 cm cake tin. Bake for 60 minutes at 160°C.

THIS IS A RECIPE FOR COOKS WHO HATE TO WEIGH INGREDIENTS – YOU JUST USE THE SOUR CREAM TUB. THE CAKE SHOULD BE MOIST AND FUDGY ON THE INSIDE.

Sarah Stevens-Gieseg of Christchurch

Blueberry and Cinnamon Teacake

MAKES AVERAGE-SIZED CAKE

300 g frozen blueberries

1½ cups plain flour

½ cup self-raising flour

1 teaspoon baking soda

250 g butter

¾ cup Chelsea caster sugar

2 eggs

300 g sour cream

¾ cup chopped walnuts

3 tablespoons Chelsea soft brown sugar

1 teaspoon cinnamon

Chelsea icing sugar for dusting

Defrost and leave blueberries to drain. Sift flours and baking soda. In a separate bowl, cream butter and caster sugar, then beat in eggs one at a time. Stir in sour cream and fold in flours. In another bowl, combine walnuts, brown sugar, cinnamon and blueberries. Put half the cake mixture in a well-greased or paper-lined large ring tin. Add the blueberry mixture, then spoon the remaining cake mixture on top. Bake for 45 minutes at 180°C. Cool for 5 minutes in the tin, then remove to a wire rack. Serve dusted with icing sugar.

Sultana and Orange Jelly Loaf

MAKES REGULAR-SIZED LOAF

2 cups boiling water
1 packet jelly orange (or lemon) flavoured
$^1/_2$ cup Chelsea white sugar
60 g butter
2 teaspoons baking soda
375 g sultanas
3 cups flour
3 teaspoons baking powder
$^1/_2$ cup chopped walnuts (optional)

Combine water, jelly crystals and sugar in a large bowl. Sir to dissolve. Add the butter, baking soda and sultanas. Stir to mix well, cover and leave overnight or at least 8 hours. Next morning add the rest of the ingredients. Mix well, and pour into one large well-greased and baking-paper-lined loaf tin. Bake for 1$^1/_4$ hours at 180°C. Cool on a wire rack.

Slice and serve buttered if desired.

JO SEAGAR'S TIPS

This is an unusual recipe that needs to be started the night before eating, but it's worth the extra effort for the wonderful flavour. Instead of making one loaf, divide into two smaller tins so you can give one away. Smaller tins may cook faster, so check after 50–60 minutes.

Alan Daken of Waihi

Banana Cake Gone Tropo

MAKES AVERAGE-SIZED CAKE

1 1/2 cups flour

1/2 teaspoon cinnamon

1/2 teaspoon nutmeg

1 teaspoon baking soda

1 cup Chelsea white sugar

3 eggs lightly beaten

1 cup buttermilk

1/2 cup chopped walnuts

1 cup sultanas

1 x 225 g can crushed pineapple pieces
  drained

2 cups over-ripe bananas mashed

Sift flour, spices, and soda into a large bowl, stir in remaining ingredients until just combined. Pour mixture into well-greased or baking-paper-lined 25 cm baking tin. Bake for 60 minutes at 180°C. Let stand for 10 minutes. Turn onto cake rack to cool. Spread with cream cheese icing.

Cream Cheese Icing

100 g cream cheese

2 cups Chelsea icing sugar

grated rind and juice of 1 lemon

Soften cream cheese, add icing sugar and grated lemon rind. Mix, adding enough lemon juice to get the right consistency to spread. Mix until smooth. Delicious served with a dollop of cream for afternoon tea.

Lesley Turner of Queenstown

Sticky Rum and Date Cake

MAKES AVERAGE-SIZED CAKE

250 g dates

1 teaspoon baking soda

1 cup boiling water

50 g butter

1/2 cup Chelsea white sugar

1/2 cup Chelsea soft brown sugar

1 egg

1/2 cup walnut pieces

1 teaspoon vanilla essence

1 1/2 cups flour

1/4 teaspoon salt

1 teaspoon mixed spice

Rum Syrup

30 g butter

1/2 cup Chelsea white sugar

1/4 cup water

1 teaspoon rum essence

Cut dates into three pieces, sprinkle with soda and cover with boiling water. Cool. Cream butter and sugars together, then add egg. Add nuts and essence, then the date mixture and mix well. Sift flour, salt and spice and fold into date mixture. (Do not over-mix.) Put into a well-greased or baking-paper-lined 23 cm cake tin. Bake for 40–45 minutes at 160°C.

When cooked, remove from oven and make the rum syrup. Boil butter, sugar, and water for 1 minute, then add essence. Pierce top of cake with a clean knitting needle or bamboo skewer and drizzle over hot syrup.

I'VE BEEN BAKING CAKES FOR OVER 50 YEARS. THIS STARTED AS A DATE LOAF BUT IS NOW VERY MUCH A CAKE. THE RUM TOPPING IS AN IDEA I TRIED FOR THIS COMPETITION AND IT REALLY WORKS WELL.

Marion Claridge of Alexandra

Cucumber Cake with Sunflower Seeds

MAKES AVERAGE-SIZED LOAF OR SMALL CAKE

125 g butter
1 cup Chelsea white sugar
2 teaspoons vanilla essence
2 eggs
1 cup flour
1 teaspoon baking powder
1 teaspoon ground cinnamon
$^1/_2$ cup sunflower seeds
1 cup of peeled grated cucumber drained

Cream butter, sugar and vanilla essence, add eggs (one at a time). Add flour, baking powder, cinnamon and sunflower seeds and fold through the grated cucumber. Spoon into a well-greased or paper-lined loaf tin. Bake for 45 minutes at 150°C. Cool on a wire rack. This is delicious as it is or can be buttered like a loaf.

THIS IS ONE OF MY FAVOURITE RECIPES FROM DENMARK. I MOVED TO NEW ZEALAND FOUR MONTHS AGO AND WOULD LIKE TO SHARE THIS LOVELY DANISH RECIPE WITH THIS COUNTRY.

Helle Smith of Waihi Beach

Pink Lady Cake

THIS IS A LOVELY
MOIST CAKE,
WHICH I ICE WITH PINK (OR
CHOCOLATE) ICING. IT WAS
MOTHER'S RECIPE. I HAVE
BEEN MAKING IT SINCE I WAS
10 YEARS OLD AND AM NOW
50, SO HAVE HAD 40
YEARS OF PINK LADY
CAKE!

MAKES AVERAGE-SIZED CAKE

250 g butter
1 cup Chelsea white sugar
1 egg
1 cup flour
$^1/_4$ cup desiccated coconut
$^1/_2$ teaspoon cochineal or pink food
*   colouring soaked in $^1/_2$ cup of milk*
1 teaspoon baking powder

Cream butter and sugar, add egg. Alternately add flour and coconut and the 'pink' milk mixture. Add baking powder and mix until smooth. Pour into a well-greased and paper-lined round or square approx. 20 cm cake tin. Bake for 35 minutes at 190°C. Cool on a wire rack and ice with pink butter icing when cold.

Pink Butter Icing

2 cups Chelsea icing sugar
25 g butter melted
1–2 drops cochineal or pink food colouring
desiccated coconut to sprinkle on top

Mix all ingredients together until a smooth creamy consistency. Sprinkle with coconut.

Kathy White of Glenfield, Auckland

Lemon Curd Cake

MAKES AVERAGE-SIZED CAKE

2 cups self-raising flour
1 cup Chelsea white sugar
100 g butter
2 eggs
2 cups lemon curd

Place flour, sugar and butter in a food processor and blend until mixture resembles fine breadcrumbs. Add eggs and mix to a soft dough. Press $^2/_3$ of dough into a well-greased or baking-paper-lined 25 cm springform cake tin. Spread lemon curd over dough and crumble small pieces of remaining dough over curd layer. Bake for 35–40 minutes at 180°C. Cool on a wire rack.

Dust with icing sugar and serve with whipped cream. Extra lemon curd can be served as a sauce.

Lemon Curd
MAKES 2 CUPS

4 large lemons
100 g butter
2 cups Chelsea white sugar
4 eggs

Finely grate lemon rind and squeeze the juice of the lemons. Place in a bowl, add butter and sugar. Place bowl over a saucepan of hot water and heat until the butter has melted. In a separate bowl beat the eggs and add to lemon mixture stirring constantly until the mixture thickens. Cool.

Ruth Day of Takaka

Taranaki A and P Show Ginger Cake

MAKES LARGE RING-CAKE

125 g butter
1 cup Chelsea white sugar
2 eggs beaten
¹/₂ cup golden syrup
1 cup milk
2 cups flour
pinch salt
1 teaspoon baking powder
2 dessertspoons ground ginger
1 teaspoon mixed spice
1 teaspoon cinnamon
1 teaspoon baking soda mixed in milk

Cream butter, sugar, add eggs, golden syrup and milk. Add remaining ingredients and mix well. Pour into a large 25 cm well-greased or baking-paper-lined ring tin. Bake for 30–45 minutes at 180°C. Cool on a wire rack. When cold, ice with ginger butter icing.

MY MOTHER WON FIRST PRIZE FOR THIS CAKE AT THE TARANAKI AGRICULTURE SOCIETY WINTER SHOW IN 1938.

Ginger Butter Icing

2 cups Chelsea icing sugar
1 teaspoon ground ginger
25 g butter melted
boiling water

Mix icing sugar, ground ginger and butter together, adding enough boiling water to make a spreadable butter icing.

Gay Leitch of Papakura, Auckland

MUFFINS

Left: Tropical Crush Muffins

A big proportion of our selected muffins are tried and true recipes, where contestants don't claim to have invented the original basic recipes but they sure have modified and perfected them with skill and style. We've included some wonderful oldies in here that stretch the definition of muffins to its delicious limit: a basic honest made-for-years ginger gem; a light-as-feather queen cake; and of course this book wouldn't be complete without the signature recipe of Chelsea buns.

According to the winner's flatmates, her Tropical Crush Muffins are the best muffins they have ever eaten and there are always arguments over who is going to eat the last one. They're gone in a flash and she's bombarded with demands for another batch!

Muffins are ideal for resourceful Kiwis because just about anything can be turned into a muffin, from passionfruit and persimmons to curried apple. Some of the recipes were specially developed to use up excess produce from the garden or to make the most of what was left in the pantry, add to that a bit of culinary wizardry and the results have been mouth-watering. We've covered the entire range and the good news is that the main characteristic of all muffin entries is true of all good muffins: quick to prepare, short cooking time and wonderful results.

Jo Seagar

Raspberry Surprise Muffins

MAKES 12

50 g butter melted
$^3/_4$ cup milk
2 eggs
1$^3/_4$ cups flour
$^1/_2$ cup Chelsea white sugar
3 teaspoons baking powder
2 teaspoons cinnamon
small tub cream cheese softened
  (approx. 150 g)
12 raspberries fresh or free-flow frozen
  (which should remain frozen)

Mix butter, milk and eggs. Add flour, sugar, baking powder and cinnamon. Fill well-greased or oil-sprayed muffin tray $^1/_3$ full with mixture. Add 1 teaspoon of cream cheese to each muffin. Place 1 fresh or frozen raspberry on top. Fill with remaining mixture and bake for 15–18 minutes at 200°C. Leave in muffin tray for 5 minutes before lifting out onto rack to cool. Dust with icing sugar if desired.

THIS IS AN ADAPTATION OF A STANDARD RECIPE. I LOVE THE TANG OF THE CREAM-CHEESE FILLING AGAINST THE SWEETNESS OF THE BERRIES. ENJOY THE SURPRISE INSIDE!

Karen Gourley of Alexandra

Cheese, Bacon and Banana Muffins

MAKES 12 REGULAR-SIZED MUFFINS

2 cups flour

1 cup Chelsea white sugar

$^1/_2$ cup parsley finely chopped

4 rashers rindless bacon finely chopped
 and cooked in microwave or frypan

2 ripe bananas mashed

1$^1/_2$ cups tasty cheese grated

2 teaspoons baking powder

3 eggs

2 cups milk

2 teaspoons dry mustard powder

150 g butter

salt and pepper to taste

Mix all ingredients until just combined. Don't overmix. Spoon mixture into well-greased or oil-sprayed muffin tray. Bake for 25-35 minutes at 160°C. Cool slightly in the tray, then remove to cool further on a wire rack.

Carolyn Bowey of Nelson

Mini After-Dinner Mint Muffins

MAKES APPROX. 24

1 ³/₄ cups flour
1 teaspoon baking soda
1 cup Chelsea white sugar
¹/₄ cup cocoa
100 g butter melted
1 egg
1 cup milk
1 teaspoon peppermint essence

Preheat oven to 200°C. Mix all ingredients until smooth. Spoon into well-greased or oil-sprayed mini muffin trays. Bake for 10 minutes. Cool slightly in the trays then remove and cool further on a wire rack.

Serve warm or cold, and if desired dust with icing sugar, or as pictured cover with melted dark chocolate.

Tessa Herbert of Whangarei

Good Old Favourite Chelsea Buns

MAKES 14–15

120 g butter
4 cups self-raising flour
$^{1}/_{2}$ teaspoon salt
$1^{1}/_{2}$ cups milk
$^{1}/_{2}$ cup Chelsea soft brown sugar
$1^{1}/_{2}$ cups mixed dried fruit (sultanas, currants etc.)
1 teaspoon cinnamon

In a food processor chop 60 g of the butter into the flour and salt. Transfer to a large bowl and mix to a firm dough with the milk. On a floured surface, roll dough out into a rectangle of about 1 cm thickness. Cream the remaining 60 g of butter with the brown sugar. Spread this onto the dough and sprinkle with the mixed dried fruit and cinnamon. Roll lengthwise so you have a long sausage. Cut into 14 or 15 slices and place on a greased or paper-lined sponge-roll tin. Bake for 30 minutes at 180°C.

Glaze
2 tablespoons water
2 tablespoons Chelsea white sugar
2 teaspoons gelatine

In a small saucepan or microwave bowl heat the above until dissolved. Brush over the cooked buns while still hot. Cool in the tin, then pull apart when cool enough to handle.

ALTHOUGH I HAVE BEEN MAKING THESE FOR YEARS, THEY ARE STILL A GREAT FAVOURITE TODAY WITH ALL MY FAMILY, FRIENDS AND VISITORS. THEY ARE MY VERSION OF A CLASSIC RECIPE.

Tropical Crush Muffins

MAKES 18

1 mashed banana

³/₄ cup passionfruit pulp (1 small jar of pulp)

1 x 225 g can crushed pineapple including juice

2 tablespoons finely chopped crystallised ginger

60 g butter melted

2 eggs

200 ml milk

1 teaspoon vanilla essence

2 cups flour

¹/₂ cup Chelsea white sugar

2 teaspoons baking powder

¹/₂ teaspoon ground ginger

¹/₂ teaspoon baking soda

pinch salt

Preheat oven to 180°C. Mix fruit together including ginger. Add butter, eggs, milk, and vanilla essence, then all the dry ingredients. Mix (but don't overmix). Spoon into 2 well-greased or oil-sprayed muffin trays. Bake for 30 minutes at 180°C, cool for a couple of minutes in trays before turning out onto a wire cooling rack. Dust with icing sugar to serve.

THEY'RE OUR PERFECT SUNDAY MORNING BRUNCH TREAT.

Mary Anne Webber of Mt Eden, Auckland

Dad's Tea Buns

MAKES 12

60 g butter
2 cups flour
2 teaspoons baking powder
$^1/_2$ cup Chelsea white sugar
1 egg
$^3/_4$ cup milk (165 ml approx.)
1 cup sultanas

Preheat oven to 220°C. Rub butter into flour, baking powder and sugar (or you can do this in the food processor). Beat egg and milk together and stir into mixture, forming a moist dough. Add the sultanas. Put tablespoonfuls on a well-greased or paper-lined tray. Sprinkle with a little extra sugar. Bake for 10 minutes at 220°C until golden brown. Cool on a wire rack. Before eating make a small cut in the top and pop in some butter.

THIS RECIPE, A FAVOURITE WITH ALL MY CHILDREN AND GRANDCHILDREN, WAS HANDED DOWN BY MY FATHER. HE USED TO BAKE A BATCH FOR PICNICS AND THAT IS WHAT THEY ARE USED FOR TO THIS DAY.

Clifford Matthews of Whitby, Wellington

Ginger Gems

MAKES **24** GEMS

100 g butter plus extra 50–60 g for the gem irons

³/₄ cup Chelsea white sugar

2 eggs

2 tablespoons Chelsea golden syrup

1¹/₂ cups flour

1 teaspoon ground ginger

¹/₂ teaspoon mixed spice

¹/₄ teaspoon baking powder

1 teaspoon baking soda

¹/₂ cup milk

whipped cream for filling

Chelsea icing sugar for dusting

Preheat oven to 200°C and place gem irons in oven to preheat while mixing ingredients. Cream 100 g of the butter and the sugar together. Add beaten eggs and golden syrup. Mix in dry ingredients and lastly the milk. Put approx. ¹/₂ teaspoon of the remaining butter in each section of the gem irons to melt, then spoon in the mixture. Bake for 15–18 minutes at 200 °C. Cool slightly in irons, then tip out on a wire rack. When completely cool, split and fill with whipped cream. Dust with icing sugar.

JO SEAGAR'S TIPS

Gem irons range in size from 12 to 24 moulds. If you have the 12 gem size, just repeat with the second portion of mixture. Because the irons rust, I find washing, then drying in a warm oven, followed by a light spray of cooking oil is the perfect way to store them.

Jean Robinson of Te Atatu, Auckland

Ginger Gems (from left) and Mrs H's Queen Cakes

Mrs H's Queen Cakes

MAKES 24

125 g butter
$^1/_2$ cup Chelsea white sugar
2 eggs beaten
$^1/_4$ cup milk
$^1/_2$ teaspoon lemon essence
1$^1/_2$ cups flour
$^1/_2$ teaspoon baking soda
1 teaspoon cream of tartar
1 cup sultanas

Cream butter and sugar. Add beaten eggs and mix well. Add milk and lemon essence alternately with dry ingredients, adding the sultanas at the end. Spoon into well-greased patty tins or muffin trays. Bake for 12 minutes at 200°C. Cool slightly in the tins, then turn out to cool further on a wire rack.

THIS WAS ONE OF MY FAVOURITES AS A YOUNG CHILD. SO QUICK AND EASY TO MAKE – THESE WERE ALWAYS IN THE TINS FOR WHEN FOLK POPPED IN FOR A CUPPA. THEY WON SECOND PRIZE AT THE NORFOLK HORTICULTURE SOCIETY ON 4 MARCH 1938.

Debbie Tatton of Takanini, Auckland

Kate's Baby Persimmon and Coconut Cakes

MAKES 30

1 large persimmon

2 cups flour

4 teaspoons baking powder

$^1/_2$ cup coconut

$^1/_2$ cup Chelsea caster sugar

100 g butter melted

2 eggs

1 cup milk

1 teaspoon coconut essence

2 extra tablespoons coconut to sprinkle

Peel and finely dice persimmon (to the size of corn kernels or peas.) Combine flour, baking powder and coconut and stir in sugar. Make a well in the centre. In another bowl mix butter, eggs, milk and coconut essence. Pour the liquid ingredients and persimmon pieces into the well and lightly combine. Spoon into greased baby muffin trays. Sprinkle with extra coconut. Bake for 10–12 minutes at 200°C. Cool in trays, then tip out onto a wire rack to cool further.

JO SEAGAR'S TIPS

Don't overbeat or use a food processor for muffins. Just lightly mix the ingredients to combine them. This will produce light, tender muffins that are smoothly rounded

Kate's Baby Persimmon and Coconut Cakes (foreground)
and Fruit Salad Muffins

Fruit Salad Muffins

MAKES 12

- 100 g butter melted
- 1 cup milk
- 1 egg
- 2 cups flour
- 4 teaspoons baking powder
- $^1/_2$ teaspoon salt
- $^1/_2$ cup Chelsea caster sugar
- 1 x 225 g can fruit salad in juice or syrup (drained)

Mix butter, milk and egg together. Add the dry ingredients and just lightly combine, don't overmix. Oil spray or grease muffin trays. Spoon mixture into trays to fill up to $^1/_3$ full. Add 1 tablespoon of fruit salad on top of mixture, then cover fruit salad with remaining mixture. Bake for 10–15 minutes at 200°C. Cool a few minutes in trays then tip out onto a wire rack to cool further.

WE HAD A THOROUGHLY ENJOYABLE 'BAKE OFF' AT SCHOOL. WE STARTED WITH OVER 50 ENTHUSIASTIC PUPILS AND I AM ONE OF THE FINALISTS.

Simon James Lucas of Whangaparaoa

Whole-Orange and Raisin Muffins

MAKES 12

1 orange quartered
$^1/_2$ cup extra orange juice
1 egg
$^1/_4$ cup oil
$^1/_2$ cup raisins
$1^1/_2$ cups flour
$^3/_4$ cups Chelsea white sugar
1 teaspoon baking powder
1 teaspoon baking soda
3 tablespoons Chelsea soft brown sugar
3 tablespoons finely chopped walnuts

Remove any pips, then process whole orange in food processor until finely chopped. Add juice, egg, oil, raisins and pulse briefly. Tip into a large bowl. Gently fold orange mixture with the remaining ingredients (except the brown sugar and walnuts) until just combined. Spoon into greased or oil-sprayed muffin tray. Sprinkle with brown sugar and walnuts mixed together. Bake for 15 minutes at 200°C. Cool a few minutes in the tray, then tip out and further cool on a wire rack.

Joy Ward of Karori, Wellington

Olive and Rosemary Muffins

MAKES 12

2 cups flour

4 teaspoons baking powder

pinch salt

$^1/_2$ cup Chelsea white sugar

$^1/_4$ cup fresh rosemary chopped

1 cup milk

1 egg

100 g butter melted

1 cup olives stones removed and roughly
    chopped

extra rosemary to sprinkle on top of
    muffins

JO SEAGAR'S TIPS

These are great served with olive tapenade and cheese. To make the tapenade, blend 2 cups of pitted olives with 2 tablespoons of olive oil and 1 teaspoon of crushed garlic. Add 2–3 tablespoons of chopped parsley.

Put dry ingredients including rosemary in bowl. In a separate bowl, mix milk and egg and beat well with melted butter. Add olives to liquids and stir. Put liquid mixture into dry ingredients and mix lightly (do not overmix). Spoon into greased muffin tray and sprinkle with extra rosemary. Bake for 12–15 minutes at 220°C. Remove from oven and stand for 2–3 minutes before cooling on a wire rack.

'Walkie Talkie' Curry Muffins

THIS RECIPE WAS VOTED MY **BEST EVER** BY THE 'WAITAKERE WALKIE-TALKIES', A GROUP WHO MEET EVERY MONDAY FOR A BUSH WALK FOLLOWED BY **COFFEE AND SNACKS**. THE TALKING DURING THE REFRESHMENTS IS AS IMPORTANT AS THE WALKING!

MAKES 12

2 cups self-raising flour
2 teaspoons baking powder
1 teaspoon curry powder
60 g butter melted
1 egg
330 g plain yoghurt
$^1/_2$ cup Chelsea white sugar
1 teaspoon lemon juice
1 green apple ie Granny Smith, cored and finely chopped (no need to peel)
$^1/_4$ cup coconut
$^1/_4$ cup sultanas

Preheat oven to 200°C. Mix all ingredients together until just combined – don't overmix. Spoon into well-greased or oil-sprayed muffin tray. Bake for 20 minutes at 200°C until golden brown. Cool a few minutes in tray and then tip out to further cool on a wire rack.

Tony Lindop of Glen Eden, Auckland

Mountain-bike Muffins

MAKES 12

1 cup Chelsea soft brown sugar
$^1/_2$ cup coconut
$1^1/_2$ cups flour
$1^1/_2$ cups breakfast cereal (Just Right,
    Bran Flakes, etc.)
3 teaspoons baking powder
2 tablespoons custard powder
$^1/_4$ cup chopped nuts
$^1/_2$ cup oil
2 tablespoons Chelsea golden syrup
1 egg beaten
1 cup milk

Place dry ingredients in bowl. In a microwave-proof jug place the oil and golden syrup. Microwave 30 seconds on high and add egg and milk. Pour into dry ingredients and stir together until just mixed. Spoon into well-greased or oil-sprayed muffin tray. Bake for 12–15 minutes at 200°C. Cool a few minutes in tray then tip out onto a wire rack to cool further.

FIRST MADE AS A **HEALTHY SNACK** FOR MY DAUGHTER'S MOUNTAIN-BIKE TRIP – HENCE THE NAME. LIVING OUT OF TOWN, I JUST HAD TO USE WHAT WAS **IN MY CUPBOARD**.

JO SEAGAR'S TIPS

Nuts are high in oils and tend to go rancid in warm temperatures. The best way to store them is in Ziplock bags in the freezer.

Diane Walker of Pukeatau, Te Awamutu

Rhubarb and Custard Muffins

MAKES 12

3 stalks rhubarb

3 tablespoons water

2 cups flour

4 teaspoons baking powder

$^{1}/_{2}$ teaspoon salt

$^{1}/_{2}$ cup custard powder

$^{1}/_{2}$ cup Chelsea white sugar

100 g butter melted

1 cup milk

1 egg beaten

Chop rhubarb into 1–2 cm pieces and microwave with water for 2 minutes (until tender but still retaining shape). In a separate bowl place flour, baking powder, salt and custard powder. Add sugar, butter, milk and egg then stir in the rhubarb and mix until just blended (don't overmix). Pour into a well-greased muffin tray. Bake for 12 minutes at 180°C. Cool a couple of minutes, then tip out onto a wire rack to cool further. If desired dust with icing sugar to serve.

PRESERVES, PICKLES & SAUCES

Left: Malaysian-style Peanut Vegetable Pickles

Turning excess produce into something that would keep became part of the early settlers' home-making art. Many of the people sending in recipes re-lived their childhood memories of collecting blackberries and strict commands to stir the bubbling pots to stop burning. Jams, jellies, pickles, sauces and relishes were all made over a hot stove, often in the middle of summer. However, by tasting time, any discomfort experienced during preparation was long forgotten and the effort deemed well worth it for the wonderful variety preserves provided to the daily diet.

Today old flavours are rediscovered and reinvented. The recipes chosen for this book range from easier and tastier ways with such Kiwi classics as beetroot pickle and tomato sauce, to recipes inspired by new flavours and ingredients from abroad. The appeal of home preserves is as great as ever. I love trapping those seasonal high notes in glass, so they can glow like heirlooms in the pantry cupboard.

Chutneys, pickles and homemade sauces not only provide the gorgeous variety we crave to liven up cold cuts or bread and cheese, but they can also shorten your 'hard-to-buy-for' list by becoming the most welcome perfect gift.

Jo Seagar

Beetroot Pickle

MAKES 4–5 CUPS

1 kg beetroot
700 g onions finely chopped (can be done
    in food processor)
$^1/_2$ teaspoon white pepper
2 teaspoons ground allspice
1 tablespoon salt
$2^1/_2$ cups Chelsea white sugar
malt vinegar approx. 500 ml
2 tablespoons cornflour

Boil the unpeeled and scrubbed beetroot
for $^3/_4$ hour. Cool, then peel and chop
finely (a food processor will make this
easy). Place in a preserving pan with the
onions, pepper, spice, salt and sugar.
Cover with malt vinegar and boil gently
for $^1/_2$ an hour. Thicken with the cornflour
mixed to a paste with a little malt vinegar.
Stir and simmer a further 10 minutes.
Bottle in clean sterilised jars and seal.

MY MOTHER GAVE ME THIS RECIPE WHEN I MARRIED
42 YEARS AGO. IT IS GREAT WITH CHEESE,
COLD MEATS, IN SANDWICHES AND AS A
DIP FOR PRE-DINNER NIBBLES.

Dorothey Jones of Whangamata

Pear Chutney

MAKES 3 MEDIUM JARS

700 g pears cored and finely chopped
4 medium onions finely chopped
1 small green pepper de-seeded and
  chopped
1 small red pepper de-seeded and chopped
4–5 medium-sized ripe tomatoes diced
2 cups Chelsea demerara sugar
1½ teaspoons salt
¼ teaspoon ground cloves
good pinch cayenne pepper
2–3 cloves garlic crushed (1 teaspoon)
450 ml malt vinegar

Place fruit and vegetables in a saucepan and cook gently, stirring frequently, with no extra liquid until soft (approx. 15 minutes). Add sugar, salt, cloves, cayenne pepper, garlic and vinegar. Bring slowly to the boil. Stir continually until sugar has dissolved. Simmer uncovered until chutney becomes thick, without excess liquid on the surface (approx. 30–40 minutes). Pour into hot sterilised jars and seal using vinegar-proof lids. Store for 2 weeks before using.

THIS RECIPE WAS AN OLD FAMILY ONE THAT HAS BEEN USED FOR YEARS.

Jeanne Newton of Napier

Sweet Pepper Relish

3 yellow peppers
3 orange peppers
3 red peppers
3 green peppers
3 purple sweet peppers
12 medium onions
3 cups Chelsea white sugar
4 cups cider vinegar
1 teaspoon mustard seeds

Wash, dry and slice the peppers. Remove seeds and white strips of flesh, reserving 1 teaspoon of pepper seeds. Finely chop peppers and onions in the food processor or with a knife. Place chopped pepper and onion in a colander or sieve inside a large bowl and pour over boiling water. Stand in the boiling water for 5 minutes, then drain, discarding water. Repeat, but stand for only 2 minutes. Drain thoroughly and place in large saucepan. Mix the remaining ingredients including reserved pepper seeds into the pepper mixture and bring to the boil. Boil for 20 minutes until glossy and thick. Place in hot sterilised jars and seal while hot.

THIS RELISH LOOKS BEAUTIFUL – LIKE JEWELS.

L. Arona of Papamoa

Blackberry and Banana Jam

MAKES 3 MEDIUM JARS

3 kg blackberries
3 kg Chelsea white sugar
1 kg over-ripe bananas

Mash blackberries in a large saucepan with a potato masher. Boil for 20 minutes over a medium heat. Add the sugar and continue to boil for 15 minutes more, then add mashed bananas. Bring to the boil and test for setting. Pour into sterilised jars, seal and label.

THIS RECIPE MUST BE AT LEAST

65 YEARS OLD

BECAUSE AS A CHILD OF 13 I USED

TO PICK BLACKBERRIES IN FRASERTOWN PADDOCKS. MY MOTHER WOULD THEN MAKE THEM INTO THIS JAM.

PRESERVES, PICKLES & SAUCES

Dorothy Bray of Waipukurau

Malaysian-style Peanut Vegetable Pickles

MAKES 4 LITRES, 2 X 2 LITRE
ICE-CREAM CONTAINERS

1³/₄ cups oil

¹/₂ cup lemon-grass stalks chopped and
   drained

3 tablespoons crushed chilli (more or less
   to taste)

1 cup chopped onions (about 3 medium
   onions)

1 cup crushed garlic

4 tablespoons turmeric (40 g packet)

1¹/₂ cups white vinegar

1¹/₂ cups Chelsea white sugar

4 teaspoons salt

4 cups carrots sliced at 2.5 cm lengths

2 cup fresh beans sliced

3 cups cauliflower florets sliced

4 cups cabbage cut 2.5 cm square pieces

2¹/₂ cups peanuts toasted and chopped
   finely

1 cup sesame seeds toasted (this can be
   easily done in the microwave)

Do not add any water at all to this recipe.

In a blender or food processor, combine just 1 cup of the oil and process lemon-grass until fine. Add chilli, onion, garlic and turmeric. Blend to a paste and pour with the rest of the oil (³/₄ cup) into a large saucepan and simmer over a medium-low heat, stirring often, for 30–40 minutes.

Add the vinegar, sugar and salt and simmer for 5 minutes. The carrots, beans and cauliflower should be dried and cut into similar-sized pieces, then added to the saucepan. Bring to the boil and cook for 5 minutes. Add the cabbage and boil for a further 5 minutes. Remove from heat.

Mix in the chopped peanuts and sesame seeds and leave to cool. Pour into covered plastic containers or screw-top jars and store in the fridge.

JO SEAGAR'S TIPS

The lemon-grass stalks, crushed chilli and crushed garlic are all available in jars in the supermarket. This is wonderful with burgers, on a cheeseboard, with B.B.Q. meats and chicken in sandwiches, pitas and with crusty breads. A real winner and so easy to make.

Stephanie Chau of Palmerston North

PRESERVES, PICKLES
& SAUCES

Roseberry Cherry Preserve

MAKES 3 MEDIUM-SIZED JARS

1 kg cherries
500 g Chelsea caster sugar
2 tablespoons lime or lemon juice
1/4 cup cherry brandy, brandy or
*   cranberry juice*
1 cup red rose petals
1 tablespoon distilled rosewater
1 x 275 g jar whole-berry cranberry jelly

A SIMPLE MICROWAVE RECIPE THAT COULD EASILY BE CONVERTED TO THE STOVETOP. THIS PRESERVE IS A GREAT WAY TO MAKE THE MOST OF THESE GORGEOUS CHERRIES. IT'S DELICIOUS ON **PANCAKES** OR **WAFFLES** OR FOR A BLACK FOREST CAKE.

Halve and stone the cherries. Place in a large microwave-proof jug. Pour in the sugar and lime or lemon juice. Leave for 2 hours or until the juices start to run. Cover loosely and microwave on high for 5 minutes. Stir in the cherry brandy, rose petals and rosewater. Microwave for 5 minutes on medium. Add the cranberry jelly. Microwave for 10 minutes on low, stopping every 2 minutes to stir. Stand until it acquires a syrup texture and starts to gel, forming a soft skin when tested on a cold saucer. Cool and ladle into jars. Store in the fridge for up to 2 months.

Jo Seagar's tips

Rosewater is made by distilling fragrant rose petals. You find it in chemists or gourmet sections of delicatessens and supermarkets.

Diane Davidson of Pt England, Auckland

Bright Red Tomato Sauce

MAKES 2 LARGE SAUCE BOTTLES

6 kg ripe red tomatoes
4 apples
2 onions
2 tablespoons allspice
2 cloves garlic (1 teaspoon crushed)
1¹/₂ kg Chelsea white sugar
¹/₄ cup salt
ground black pepper
1 litre malt vinegar

Wash and chop tomatoes and apples, skins included. Chop onions. Tie allspice and garlic in a muslin bag. Boil all ingredients together slowly for two hours, stirring frequently. When cool, discard muslin bag and put sauce through a sieve, or use a food processor. Bottle in warm sterilised bottles when cool.

THIS IS A TRULY OLD FAVOURITE RECIPE THAT HAS BEEN **PASSED DOWN** AND AROUND IN THE FAMILY FOR ABOUT FIFTY YEARS. IT'S JUST SO **EASY PEASY!**

Janet Russell of Browns Bay, Auckland

Enid's Prize Marmalade

MAKES 3 MEDIUM JARS

8 oranges
4 lemons
to each 500 g of fruit add 1.2 litres water
for every cup of pulp add 1 cup Chelsea
white sugar

Cut fruit finely, then place in a pan with the water. Boil for 30 minutes, then leave for 24 hours. Add the sugar and soak for 1 hour. Boil for 30 minutes, then simmer for about another 15 minutes until it sets when tested on a cold saucer. Place in warmed sterilised jars and cover.

AS A CHILD I REMEMBER NANA MAKING HER MARMALADE ON HER OLD CAST-IRON OVEN. MY JOB WAS TO GIVE IT A STIR WHEN TOLD. ANYONE VISITING NANA ALWAYS LEFT WITH A JAR.

Debbie Tatton of Takanini, Auckland

Dried Apricot, Passionfruit & Pumpkin Jam (foreground) and Passionfruit Jam

Dried Apricot, Passionfruit & Pumpkin Jam

MAKES 3 MEDIUM JARS

250 g dried apricots chopped

4 cups water

400 g chopped pumpkin (approx. 3 cups finely diced)

1 kg Chelsea white sugar

$^{1}/_{2}$ cup lemon juice

$^{1}/_{2}$ cup passionfruit pulp (or substitute with a small can of crushed pineapple)

Soak chopped apricots in water overnight. In the same water boil apricots and pumpkin for 20 minutes. Add sugar and boil for 25 minutes. Add lemon juice and passionfruit. Boil for 5 minutes. Bottle while hot in sterilised jars. Cover when cold.

THIS GOOD CHEAP PRESERVE SELLS LIKE HOT CAKES ON CHARITY STALLS. IT LOOKS BEAUTIFUL IN THE JARS.

Yvonne Breckcon of Birkenhead, Auckland

Passionfruit Jam

MAKES 3 MEDIUM JARS

pulp of 6 passionfruit

1 tablespoon fresh lemon juice

2 eggs

1 teaspoon butter

1 cup Chelsea white sugar

Whisk all the ingredients together. Place in a small double boiler and cook over a steady heat, stirring regularly until it thickens (approx. 35 minutes). Pour into clean sterilised jars, cover and store in the fridge.

THIS IS AN OLD RECIPE GIVEN TO ME BY A FRIEND YEARS AGO. IT IS VERY LIKE A CURD.

Claudette Blyth of Manurewa

Roasted Golden-Queen Peach Chutney

MAKES 3 MEDIUM JARS

500 g roasted peaches and juice (see below)

1 large onion roughly chopped

3 cloves garlic (1 teaspoon crushed)

1 red chilli finely sliced

$1/2$ cup Chelsea soft brown sugar

$1/2$ cup cider vinegar

grated rind and juice of 1 lemon

100 g dates

100 g sultanas

100 g glacé ginger

$1/2$ teaspoon ground cinnamon

$1/2$ teaspoon ground cardamom

Mix all the ingredients except the cinnamon and cardamom and leave overnight in a covered glass or china bowl. Add the cinnamon and cardamom, mixing well. Bake for $1^1/2$–2 hours at 180°C, stirring regularly. Try not to break up the peach segments too much, although this does happen. Remove when thick, glossy and starting to caramelise (watch carefully). Spoon into sterilised jars and seal. Leave at least 1 week before eating. Store in fridge when opened.

IN SEASON I OVEN-ROAST GOLDEN-QUEEN PEACHES, PEELED AND STONED, SPRINKLED WITH SUGAR, FOR ABOUT 2 HOURS AT 150°C (FOR 500 G, OR ABOUT 8 LARGE PEACHES, I USE 1 CUP CHELSEA WHITE SUGAR). THEN I FREEZE THE PEACHES FOR LATER USE IN SUCH DISHES AS THIS DELICIOUS CHUTNEY.

Judy Doyle of Wairoa

*Roasted Golden-Queen Peach Chutney (front left)
and Nana Alexander's Curried Pickled Onions*

Nana Alexander's Curried Pickled Onions

MAKES 2–3 BIG JARS

3 tablespoons salt
$2^1/_2$ kg pickling onions peeled
500 g Chelsea white sugar
2 tablespoons Chelsea golden syrup
1 tablespoon allspice
1 tablespoon ground cloves
1 teaspoon dried mustard powder
1 tablespoon curry powder
3 litres malt vinegar
$2^1/_2$ tablespoons cornflour

A **TREASURED**, OLD, FAMILY RECIPE THAT IS NEVER NORMALLY DISCLOSED! IT IS REALLY **SIMPLE** BUT REALLY **SCRUMMIE!**

Sprinkle salt over the pickling onions and cover with cold water. Stand for 24 hours. Strain and then pack tightly into jars. Put all remaining ingredients except cornflour into a heavy-bottomed saucepan and bring to the boil. Boil for 2 minutes. Mix cornflour to a paste with cold water, then stir into the mixture. Reduce heat and stir until thickened. Pour into jars, covering onions completely. Leave for at least 3 weeks before eating.

Mandy Alexander of Pauanui

Tamarillo Jam

MAKES 2 CUPS

6 plump tamarillos
2 cups water
4 cups Chelsea white sugar

Cut fruit in half. Place in a large saucepan with the water. Bring to the boil. Remove tamarillo skins and return fruit to water. Simmer for 5 minutes. Mash fruit, add the sugar and boil again for 10 minutes. Stir frequently and test for setting, then cool slightly. Pour into sterilised jars and seal.

THIS IS MY OWN RECIPE, AS I COULDN'T FIND ONE WHEN I WANTED TO USE UP SURPLUS FRUIT.

Ruth McClymont of Te Atatu, Auckland

Lime Relish with Kaffir Lime Leaves

MAKES 3 MEDIUM JARS

1 kg limes
2 onions chopped finely
1 tablespoon salt
3 cooking apples peeled and chopped
400 ml cider vinegar
1 teaspoon ground ginger
1 cup raisins
2 ¼ cups Chelsea white sugar
8 kaffir lime leaves

Cut limes in half then quarters lengthways. Cut ends off and slice thinly. Bring to boil: limes, onions, salt, apples, vinegar, ginger and raisins. Simmer 60 minutes. De-vein the lime leaves, fold in half and slice very thinly into strips. Stir the sugar and sliced leaves into the mix. Simmer for a further 30 minutes until thick. Pour into hot sterilised jars and seal.

JO SEAGAR'S TIPS

This is a wonderful Persian-style, marmalade-flavoured relish, a perfect accompaniment for spicy curries or with big hunks of cheese and French bread.

Lesley Keen of Avondale, Auckland

Dill Chokos

MAKES ABOUT 5 JARS

$^1/_2$ cup plain salt
$^1/_2$ cup Chelsea white sugar
7 cups boiling water
3 cups wine vinegar
1 large dill sprig or dill flowerhead
1 tablespoon dill seeds
3 peppercorns
1 large clove garlic
freshly picked baby chokos, 4–8 cm
    enough to fill 5 large jars, approx. 100

Prepare brine by dissolving salt and sugar in boiling water. Add vinegar and keep mixture hot. Put dill sprig and seeds, peppercorns and garlic in sterilised jars. Leave the tiny chokos whole and halve or quarter the larger ones. Add them to the jars. Pour the hot pickling mixture over chokos, leaving 1 cm at top of jars. Microwave individual jars at medium-high for 6 minutes. Place lids on and tighten, then leave to cool. Store for 2 weeks before using and make sure they are refrigerated before serving.

ALWAYS CRISP AND TASTY, THESE CHOKOS ARE ESPECIALLY NICE WITH HAM, BACON OR CORNED BEEF AND WHEREVER GERKINS ARE GOOD.

Cath Ferguson of Kerikeri

DESSERTS

Left: Crusted Butterscotch Apple Sponge

Nothing says celebration better than a spectacular dessert, and we have got something to suit everyone in this section, covering the vast range from light fluffy cheesecake to white chocolate with berries and a new way of cooking rhubarb. These recipes will suit all sizes and shapes of households with the Tiny Bread 'n' Butter Pudding for One for treating just yourself, an Easy Peasy Pudding 'n' Pie that's perfect for working parents to whizz up for the kids, and frosted grapes to add elegant sophistication to that important dinner party.

Some of the oldest recipes travelled out from Ireland and Scotland with early pioneering families. It's wonderful to see that desserts like Plum Duff are still lovingly prepared by new generations of those families, year after year. We are privileged to be able to share such treasured recipes.

With today's busy lifestyles and the need for convenient food – quick to prepare and quick to disappear – there often emerges a strong yearning for what was best in our past. Frequently, I hear people reminiscing about bubbling hot spicy puddings with lashings of cream as the single missing item that really encapsulates the comfort of their childhoods. There are some lovely old-fashioned desserts included in this section, but we've updated their preparation and presentation for contemporary tastes.

Most of us adore desserts. Eat only a little, occasionally, and you'll enjoy them even more is a great philosophy to take, but then again, how about second helpings all around!

Jo Seagar

Pears in Meringue

MAKES 6–8

6–8 ripe pears peeled but left whole with
stalks intact
4¹/₂ cups approx. apple juice
6 egg whites
2 cups Chelsea white sugar

Cook pears in apple juice until tender but firm. Slice off the bottom of each pear so they can stand in an oven dish well spaced. Whisk egg whites until stiff. Beat in 1 tablespoon of the sugar at a time until smooth and glossy. Place mixture in piping bag and pipe around each pear, starting from the base and working upwards. You can leave the stalk poking out of the meringue. Bake for 30–40 minutes at 130°C until meringue is crisp and a pale golden colour.

Serve hot or cold with whipped cream or ice-cream.

JO SEAGAR'S TIPS

Egg whites freeze really well. The ice tray makes an ideal container – one egg white per section. If you mix them, an average egg white is 60 ml.

THIS RECIPE WAS FROM AN OLD AUNT WHO DIED IN 1979.

Pineapple Shortcake

MAKES 6–8 GOOD-SIZED SERVINGS

Bring pineapple and its liquid to boil in saucepan, thicken with the custard powder and water combined. Cool. In a food processor, cream butter and sugar, add egg and sifted dry ingredients, except the extra flour. Remove half the dough, press into a shallow sponge-roll tin and spread with the cooled pineapple filling. Add extra flour to remaining dough in processor, pulsing until mixture crumbles. Sprinkle over pineapple filling, pressing down gently. Bake for 25–30 minutes at 180°C.

When cooked, dust with icing sugar, serve warm or cold with cream or ice-cream.

1 x 455 g can crushed pineapple in juice or syrup (2 cans if you want a richer filling)

3 tablespoons custard powder

$^1/_4$ cup water

125 g butter

$^3/_4$ cup Chelsea white sugar

1 egg

$^1/_4$ cup cornflour

1$^1/_2$ cups flour

1 teaspoon baking powder

extra $^1/_4$ cup flour approx.

THIS IS ADAPTED FROM MY LATE **MOTHER'S ORIGINAL** RECIPE, WHICH WAS ACCEPTED FOR PUBLICATION IN THE *NEW ZEALAND RADIO AND TELEVISION COOKBOOK*, 1974.

Joy Ward of Karori, Wellington

Crusted Butterscotch Apple Sponge

MAKES 4–6 SERVINGS

MY GREAT-GRANDMOTHER WOULD MAKE HUGE ROASTING PANS FULL OF A VERSION OF THIS RECIPE USING **FRESH** APPLES FOR HER 14 CHILDREN.

3 cups (or 1 large can) chunky lightly
  stewed apple, not too wet
2 tablespoons Chelsea soft brown sugar
1 teaspoon caramel essence (or vanilla)
3 eggs
$^3/_4$ cup Chelsea caster sugar
6 tablespoons self-raising flour sifted

Preheat oven to 180°C. Thoroughly grease a 21 cm square 6 cm deep oven dish or 4–6 individual ramekins. Place apples in dish or ramekins, sprinkle with brown sugar and caramel essence, stirring to mix through. Beat eggs, adding caster sugar slowly until thick and creamy. Gently fold in flour. Pour sponge mixture over apples. Bake for 45–55 minutes at 180°C for the large dish and approximately 30–35 minutes for individual ramekins.

Dust with icing sugar and serve with softly whipped cream. Peaches, plums, apricots or berries can be substituted in this versatile pudding and you can flavour it with cinnamon, vanilla essence or nutmeg.

Bernice Morton of Invercargill

Tiny Bread 'n' Butter Puddy for One

MAKES 1

2 thin slices bread
1 tablespoon sultanas
³/₄ cup milk
1 egg
1 tablespoon Chelsea white sugar
¹/₂ teaspoon vanilla essence
cinnamon

Cut the bread into small pieces and place with the sultanas in a small baking dish. Beat milk, egg, sugar and vanilla essence together. Pour over the bread and sprinkle with cinnamon. Bake at 180°C for 20–25 minutes until the custard is set.

Serve with a little cream or ice-cream.

A DELICIOUS
OLD-FASHIONED WEE
DESSERT FOR ONE.

Jenny Blakeborough of Manurewa, Auckland

Frosted Grapes

MAKES APPROX. 10 SMALL BUNDLES

500 g grapes (preferably mixture of black, green and red)
2 egg whites
1 cup approx. Chelsea caster sugar

Wash grapes and allow to dry. Snip into small clusters. Whisk egg whites until they run off the whisk in a thin stream; they should remain clear and foamy, not stiffly beaten. Place caster sugar in its own shallow bowl. Dip each grape cluster into the egg, shaking off excess. Next dip the grapes in the caster sugar and place on an oven tray covered with greaseproof paper. Leave in warm place to dry.

The grapes can be prepared 2 or 3 weeks before use and be kept in airtight bags in the freezer.

JO SEAGAR'S TIPS

These are really special as a garnish on a pavlova or cheesecake or served as a nibble with coffee. They look far more complicated than they are and are really impressive. Other fruits like cherries and plums can be substituted.

Bliss

MAKES 4–6

125 g butter
1/2 cup Chelsea white sugar
2 tablespoons Chelsea golden syrup
1 1/2 cups flour
1 1/2 tablespoons cocoa
1 1/2 teaspoons baking powder
3/4 cup rolled oats
approx. 180 g large bar white chocolate
   (chopped into irregular chunks)
1 1/2 cups frozen berries (boysenberries or
   loganberries are best)
plain unsweetened yoghurt to serve

Grease a 24 cm round pie dish (or equivalent). Preheat oven to 180°C. In a large saucepan melt the butter, sugar and golden syrup. Add the flour, cocoa and baking powder, then stir in the rolled oats. Mix lightly. Add the chopped chocolate and whole frozen berries and carefully mix – lightly but evenly. Turn mixture out into the greased dish and bake in the oven for 15 minutes. The mixture should have puffed up slightly but still be moist.

Serve with plain, unsweetened yoghurt to counter the rich flavour. Must be served warm – straight from the oven – for maximum bliss!

MY DESSERT OF CHOICE– SMOOTH, WARM CHOCOLATE, MOIST BUT WITH A BITE AND OATY CRUNCH TOPPED BY THE FRESH TART FLAVOUR OF THE BERRIES.

JO SEAGAR'S TIPS

Chocolate should be stored in a cool dry place and be tightly wrapped. Warm temperatures cause it to bloom or turn dusty grey and mottled. This is caused by the cocoa butter rising to the surface. It doesn't affect the flavour, just its looks.

Ange Gregory of Wellington

Blackberry Dessert Cake

100 g butter
1 cup Chelsea white sugar
1 egg
1 teaspoon baking soda
1 cup milk
1^1/$_2$ cups flour
1 teaspoon cinnamon
approx. 1^1/$_2$ cups blackberries (blueberries
  or boysenberries)

Cream butter and sugar together, then add egg and beat well. Dissolve baking soda in the milk. To the creamed butter mixture, mix flour and cinnamon alternatively with the milk and soda mixture. Lastly stir in the berries. Spoon into a well-greased or paper-lined large cake tin or sponge-roll tin. Bake for 45 minutes at 190°C.

Serve warm, cut into slices and dusted with icing sugar, softly whipped cream or accompanied with ice-cream.

THIS RECIPE GOES BACK TO MY DAYS PICKING WILD BLACKBERRIES AS A CHILD. SUBSTITUTING BLUEBERRIES OR BOYSENBERRIES IS JUST AS NICE.

Fay Dwyer of Hamilton

Sue's Sour Cream and Apricot Dessert Cake

MAKES LARGE DESSERT CAKE

75 g butter melted

3 eggs

1½ teaspoons vanilla essence

¾ cup Chelsea caster sugar

¼ cup milk

2¼ cups flour

3 teaspoons baking powder

1 x 425 g can apricot halves

Melt butter, add eggs, vanilla essence, sugar and milk. Beat until light and fluffy. Fold in the flour and baking powder. Spoon into a well-greased 20 cm round cake tin with the base lined with baking paper. Arrange apricot halves on top. Bake for 25 minutes at 180°C, then remove from oven and add topping.

Topping

½ cup sour cream

1 egg

1 tablespoon Chelsea white sugar

1 teaspoons of cinnamon

Mix sour cream and egg together and spoon over hot cake. Mix sugar and cinnamon and sprinkle over top. Return to oven and cook for 10–12 minutes until set.

Serve warm with softly whipped cream or ice-cream.

JO SEAGAR'S TIPS

Canned peaches, plums, etc., can be substituted for the apricots. To really impress, serve with whipped cream and apricot jam.

Susan-Leigh Hamilton of Parparaumu

Easy Peasy Pudding 'n' Pie

MAKES 6 SERVINGS

4 eggs
1 cup Chelsea white sugar
120 g butter melted
2 teaspoons grated lemon rind
³/₄ cup coconut
³/₄ cup (120 g) ground almonds
juice 1 lemon
juice 1 orange
¹/₂ cup flour
250 g sour cream

Preheat oven to 180°C. Grease a 20 cm pie dish. Blend all ingredients in a food processor. Pour into the pie dish and place in oven. Cook for 35 minutes or until golden and set.

Serve sprinkled with icing sugar. Serve warm with cream and lemon curd – see page 46 – (for a fancy occasion) or cold (for a picnic or school lunches). You can replace sour cream with milk or yoghurt, or leave out ground almonds and add more coconut. Add essences, passionfruit pulp, cocoa – whatever you have in stock.

AS A BUSY WORKING MUM, I FIND THIS IS A GREAT DESSERT. IT TASTES LIKE A CHEESECAKE BUT WITHOUT THE FUSS.

Carol Walker of Glen Eden, Auckland

Macaroon Peaches

6 peaches cut in half and stones removed

2 tablespoons brandy (or liquor of your
   choice or orange juice)

3 egg whites

1$^1/_4$ cup Chelsea white sugar

3 teaspoons cornflour

$^1/_2$ teaspoon vanilla essence

1 teaspoon malt vinegar

1$^1/_2$ cups desiccated coconut

Lay peaches in bottom of pie dish. Pour brandy or chosen liquor on top and allow to permeate by leaving for 2 hours. In a separate bowl, beat egg whites until stiff. Add sugar gradually, combining well. Beat in the cornflour, vanilla essence and vinegar. Finally fold in coconut. Spoon or pipe coconut mixture on top of peaches. Bake at 200°C for about 20 minutes until golden brown.

Serve hot with whipped cream or thick yoghurt.

JO SEAGAR'S TIPS

If you break a piece of egg shell into the bowl when separating, it's extremely difficult to remove with a spoon or finger – the easiest solution is to use another piece of egg shell.

Peach Melba Meringue Shortcake

SERVES 6

1¹/₂ cups flour
2 teaspoons baking powder
³/₄ cup Chelsea soft brown sugar
100 g butter melted
2 egg yolks lightly beaten
¹/₂ cup sour cream
1 x 410 g can sliced peaches
1 cup free-flow frozen raspberries
3 egg whites
¹/₄ cup Chelsea caster sugar
¹/₂ cup sliced almonds

Preheat oven to 190°C. Sift flour and baking powder into large bowl. Make a well in the centre, add brown sugar, butter, egg yolks and sour cream. Mix well to form soft dough. Spread mixture evenly over the base of a lightly greased or baking-paper-lined 25 cm springform cake tin. Drain peaches thoroughly and arrange together with raspberries on top, press down gently. Bake for 20 minutes.

For the meringue topping, whisk the egg whites to the floppy soft-peak stage, add the sugar a tablespoon at a time, whisking until the mixture is stiff. Remove shortcake from oven, pile meringue over fruit, spreading right to the rim. Sprinkle with sliced almonds. Return the dish to the oven. Turn off heat and leave in the closed cooling oven for a further 30 minutes.

ALTHOUGH PEACH MELBA IS A POPULAR DESSERT FLAVOUR, MY USE OF THIS COMBO IN A MERINGUE-TOPPED SHORTCAKE IS, I BELIEVE, UNIQUE.

Diane Davidson of Pt England, Auckland

Hazelnut Torte

MAKES LARGE DESSERT

6 egg whites

2 cups Chelsea caster sugar

1½ cups chopped hazelnuts (skins removed)

48 small plain water crackers crushed to crumbs (eg. plain Snax)

300 ml cream

½ cup chopped dark chocolate

¼ cup extra chopped hazelnuts

Beat egg whites until stiff. Gradually add sugar a spoonful at time until thick and glossy. Fold in hazelnuts and biscuit crumbs. Spoon onto 2 baking-paper-lined well-greased 23 cm springform cake tins. Bake for 30–40 minutes at 160°C until crisp and dry.

Cool in the tin and then carefully remove and fill with whipped cream. Spread more cream over the top and sprinkle with the chopped chocolate and extra chopped hazelnuts.

JO SEAGAR'S TIPS

To remove hazelnut skins, place nuts in an oven dish, such as a small roasting pan. Bake at 180°C for 8–10 minutes. Tip into a clean tea-towel and rub off the skins.

| DESSERTS

Self-Saucing Ginger Toffee Pudding

MAKES 4 SERVINGS

Batter

1 cup flour

2 teaspoons baking powder

2 teaspoons ground ginger

$^1/_4$ cup Chelsea soft brown sugar

$^1/_4$ cup Chelsea white sugar

50 g butter

1 tablespoon Chelsea golden syrup

$^1/_2$ cup milk

Sauce

$^1/_2$ cup Chelsea soft brown sugar

$^1/_2$ cup Chelsea white sugar

1 tablespoon Chelsea golden syrup

2 teaspoons ginger

2 cups boiling water

Combine dry batter ingredients in a large bowl. Melt butter with golden syrup. Pour into dry ingredients with milk and mix. Place in greased oven-proof dish that is quite deep, such as a small lasagne dish.

Put sauce ingredients in a bowl (you can use the same one you used for the batter). As you add the boiling water, stir until ingredients are mostly dissolved, then pour over the batter mixture. Bake for 45 minutes at 180°C.

Serve with vanilla ice-cream or whipped

THIS IS AN ADAPTATION OF A CHOCOLATE PUDDING RECIPE, BROUGHT ABOUT ONE NIGHT WHEN I HAD NO COCOA. IT IS SO QUICK TO PREPARE – READY IN THE TIME IT TAKES TO BOIL THE JUG!

Karen Thwaites of Invercargill

Bub's Lemon Cheesecake

MAKES 6–8 SERVINGS

1 packet plain wine or digestive biscuits
crumbled (easily done in a food
processor)
125 g butter melted
1 packet lemon jelly
³/4 cup boiling water
grated rind and juice of 1 lemon
400 g cream cheese
³/4 cup Chelsea white sugar
375 ml can evaporated milk well chilled
(keep in fridge overnight)
1 teaspoon vanilla essence

Mix crushed biscuit crumbs and melted butter. Press into the base of a 21 cm springform well-greased cake tin. Bake for 10 minutes at 150°C. Cool.

Melt jelly in boiling water. Add rind and juice of the lemon. Beat the cream cheese with the sugar, add to jelly, stirring until well combined and creamy smooth. In a separate bowl, whip chilled milk until thick and fold into mixture. Add vanilla essence. Pour into crumb base and put in fridge for at least 4 hours, preferably overnight.

JO SEAGAR'S TIPS

To serve, carefully remove from tin and decorate with piped cream and fresh fruit. Kiwifruit, pineapple and passionfruit are a delicious combination or strawberries, drizzled with melted strawberry jam. Yum!

Jenny McLaughlin of Woodend

Caramel Crusted Rhubarb Pudding

MAKES **4** SERVINGS

$^3/_4$ cup flour

1 teaspoon baking powder

$^1/_2$ cup rolled oats

$^3/_4$ cup Chelsea white sugar

100 g butter melted

4 cups diced rhubarb stalks

$^3/_4$ cup Chelsea soft brown sugar

1 tablespoon cornflour

$^1/_4$ cup boiling water

Sift flour and baking powder into a bowl. Add rolled oats and white sugar, then mix in melted butter to make crust mixture. Put diced rhubarb into a greased ovenproof dish, such as a small lasagne dish or deep pie plate. Sprinkle crust mixture evenly over rhubarb. In the discarded bowl, combine brown sugar and cornflour. Spoon over crust mixture. Carefully pour the boiling water over the top. Do not stir. Bake for 30 minutes at 180°C.

Serve with custard or cream and if desired dust with icing sugar.

THE SAME LOVELY RECIPE HANDED DOWN THROUGH TWO DIFFERENT FAMILIES.

Tracey Thompson of Te Awamutu & Jennifer Charman of Christchurch

Nana Kilgour's Christmas Plum Duff

MAKES BIG FAMILY-SIZED PUDDING OR 2 SMALL ONES

2 cups flour

1 cup fresh breadcrumbs

150 g grated butter

750 g mixed fruit, raisins, currants, sultanas

2 teaspoons Chelsea treacle

1 egg

1 cup of Chelsea white sugar

pinch salt

1 teaspoon spice

1 teaspoon baking soda

milk (sufficient to mix ingredients to a stiff dough)

NAN'S FAMILY, WHO SETTLED IN OTAGO IN THE MID-1840s, BROUGHT THIS RECIPE WITH THEM FROM SCOTLAND. SEVEN GENERATIONS LATER, IT'S STILL A FAMILY FAVOURITE.

Have on hand a clean old tea-towel, string and deep saucepan of boiling water. Mix all the ingredients to a stiff dough, then spoon onto the tea-towel. Draw the edges of the tea-towel up and gently shape to a round ball. Tie the top firmly with string. Lower wrapped dough into the boiling water and boil for 3 hours, topping up the water as needed. Drain, cool, then slip silver coins wrapped in foil into the pudding just before serving. Serve while still warm or reheat in boiling water or the microwave and accompany with plain cream.

JO SEAGAR'S TIPS

The best way to let the pudding set and cool is to lift the bundle from the pan and tie the string at its top to a wooden spoon placed over an empty saucepan. Suspending the plum duff will preserve its nice round pudding shape. It will keep well in the fridge or freezer, wrapped in foil.

Jeanette Sutherland of Manukau City

Index